OUT OF REACH

Foxes like rabbits,

but sometimes rabbits are safe in their burrows.

Bears like honey,

but sometimes honey
is much too high.

Spiders like flies,

but sometimes flies fly away.

Giraffes like juicy leaves,

but sometimes the leaves are just out of reach.

Owls like mice,

but sometimes mice are hiding.

but I make sure my goldfish are safe and sound.

My cat never really misses out, though…

because he has me to feed him.